ARMEIKA
UMNIYA NAJAER

Published by Akashic Books

ISBN: 978-1-61775-640-5

Printed in China through Four Colour Print Group, Louisville, Kentucky
First printing

Akashic Books
Brooklyn, New York, USA
Ballydehob, Co. Cork, Ireland
Twitter: @AkashicBooks
Facebook: AkashicBooks
E-mail: info@akashicbooks.com
Website: www.akashicbooks.com

African Poetry Book Fund
Prairie Schooner
University of Nebraska
110 Andrews Hall
Lincoln, Nebraska 68588

Table of Contents

Preface
by Aracelis Girmay

In her biography, Umniya Najaer is described as being interested in "writing that deals with oral history and documentation." And the poems of *Armeika* are lyric docupoems written in various voices of the U.S. Sudanese diaspora. These histories and words are grounded in people, in bodies. And it is through these bodies—their particular places, hungers, joys, metaphors, and sorrows—that Najaer documents Sudan's sociopolitical history, including its history of colonialism and civil war, but also its history of water and taste, as well as the histories a body carries into its most intimate practices and hours. In this way, Najaer's work is subtle, nuanced, and very much driven by the specific and idiosyncratic languages of her speakers, among them mothers, a niece, an *I* who returns home and an *I* who leaves. Oftentimes these speakers address a beloved *you*, which is one of the ways that these poems, while tracing severances and trauma, are quietly tremendous love poems that reinforce and insist on the power of kinship and intimacy even within the context of violence and trauma.

Formally inventive and ambitious, the poems shape-shift across pages in ways that conjure migration, transience, and a regard for multiplicities. Najaer begins her collection with a swift and etymological poem-note on the single word of her title, "Armeika." And for those of us who didn't know, we soon find out that this word is really the brackish result of two words, a route that reveals the elision of the Arabic "armeik" and "amreika" (as in "America") to produce the "Armeika" of her title, a term she describes as being "used in the US-based Sudanese diaspora to imply that [the country] will toss/fling/throw / dispose of one." It is immediately clear to me that not only is Najaer offering a translation and context for her title, she is also signaling that she has imagined an audience for these poems, an audience for whom this kind of translation may or may not be necessary. In this way, Najaer establishes that her eyes are on multiple subjects, her readers among them, and that distance and translation (across languages, places, memories) are among her themes. She pulls language into the center of the lens, asking readers to consider the ways it might reflect the limitations and capacities of subjects who move between Sudanese Arabic and Sudanese English, suggesting that invention and play are present even at the site of the wound. This being a book of poems, readers must then consider the ways that the poems themselves are strategies for repair, operating within and through exile and loss.

Ultimately *Armeika* is a collection scaled to the human body. Even the city of Omdurman is described in terms of the human body as we see in the poem titled "in a truck climbing the left ventricle of omdurman's heart, three girls; two cut, one uncut." In this poem, which Najaer considers the personal histories of the subjects and female circumcision, what might it mean for the author to imagine the city's body alongside those of the three girls? Perhaps one of the things this depiction of the city's heart does is make the city and the girls kin. After all, this poem forces readers to consider the anatomy of the city alongside the anatomy of the girls. Perhaps such a title, then, pushes readers to consider the ways that this place and these girls are written with history, vast yet subject, sites of construction, deconstruction, and battle, imagined toward and into. Associative thinking gets us here. And part of what makes this work so breathtaking is how intricately and dexterously its author braids multiple hairs of possibility into any given text without ever summarizing the poem toward arrival. It is difficult to say where a body ends or begins, or if these terms are entirely useful ways to think about such bodies:

> what no one remembers:
> which one of us; you, or she, or I,
> laid splayed open on the operating table
>
> when Amu ran through the door yelling, shaking

the two others having already been cut,
red wool crossing & uncrossing at our feet

There are moments like these, in which a full answer to the question of
the poem is never granted or the details of the *I* is withheld, that we realize
the extent to which kin and place are intricately bound and, perhaps, to
each other. A history, it splinters out through various people, places, and
voices, as though light through a prism.

Najaer's work often suggests resolution while simultaneously resisting
it. Her use of line, line break, and lists imbue her poems with a disarmingly
transient physicality, as if the poems were folding in on themselves and
then unfolding out into multiple possibilities. Among the results of such
a tendency is the transference of emotional anticipation onto the reader
whom might find herself anticipating resolution where there is none, thus
developing an invested relationship to both chaos and control. We see this
in "beit fundurq masr al-khaliq ghost house":

the story goes, not long after he is buried,
neighbors begin to hear strange sounds in the night

a wail, a sob, a shriek blooming in the shadow
of a whip, a sniff, a whimper

This procession of sounds ("a wail, a sob, a shriek…") is straightforward
and, thus, grounding, even as they signal bodies in distress. But then the list
turns swiftly into the realm of image: "a shriek blooming in the shadow / of
a whip, a sniff, a whimper." And it is with this turn that time is suspended
long enough for sound to turn into not only the image of the whip's shadow,

but the act of the whipping. And so the violence spreads in slow-motion over two couplets as a result of a kind of meaningful disorientation that troubles time. This troubled time conjures the speaker's slow realization that the sounds from the neighbor's home aren't the haunting sounds of the dead husband's ghost but are, instead, the sounds of torture—the living turning the living into living ghosts. In this case, line and syntax allow the reader to experience both the shock of the realization and the lag in its unfolding. Such formal choices do not seem disconnectedly self-conscious but, instead, seem built out of the elusiveness of memory and, perhaps, the *sound* of remembering, recalling. All of this is to say that in this collection you will find concision and imagination born out of a deep commitment to, and regard for, her family, her subjects. Here is a writer who is as sharp as she is imaginative. Language is simultaneously clipped and lush. Her images are woven with distance, sobbing, rain, river, sea. Joy is "brown & streaked."

The poems themselves, filled up with potent and everyday objects (many of them repeated), become ceremonies of lasting, even as she documents hostilities and erasure. I am profoundly interested in anything this poet writes, for she writes with the tenderness and devoted attention of someone who has spent a long time studying closely the ways people lose and carry home.

armeik: **v.** present tense; to throw you;

armeik, as a threat: i will throw you down / away / dispose of you;

armeik, as a question: should i throw you down / away / dispose of you;

amreika, noun: **n.** america, also referring to the united states;

* * *

armeika: **v. or n.** combines armeik & amreika.

armeika is a term i have heard used in the US-based Sudanese diaspora to imply that the country will toss/fling/throw / dispose of one.

beit fundurq masr al-khaliq ghost house

before it was a ghost house[*] it
was the home of an old widower

the story goes, not long after he is buried,
neighbors begin to hear strange sounds in the night

a wail, a sob, a shriek blooming in the shadow
of a whip, a sniff, a whimper

neighbors think it is the widower's spirit
or a cat giving birth night after night

perhaps stray dogs nested
in the kitchen, but could it be

closer to sobbing?
no, no it must be nothing.

on certain nights when the sky fills
with voices from the widower's house,

the neighbors say,
this is no work of the devil iblis,

even he was an angel once.
whatever the crying is, supernatural or not,
it is certainly a bad omen

---

[*] Ghost houses, or *biyout al-ashbah,* are the Sudanese security apparatuses and government's illegal torture sites. The survivors say these are sites where the human spirit is severed from the body, where people are transformed into living ghosts.

none of our business, better to keep a distance.

eventually the truth comes out:

bashir's security apparatus repurposed the
widower's home, converted the master bedroom

into the site of *al-hafla*, the storage room into a cell,
the children's play area into a mock execution ground

the widower's home is the site of your torture, not only a place
that houses violence, but is itself a weapon

the ground splits your cranium, the walls usher
the lung's blood

& phlegm from the esophagus' pink flesh,
the soil is a towel absorbing feces, blood,

tears, semen, the ceiling holds the weight of you,
the rope of her arms, braided into your neck,

bloated, the verandah becomes a burial site
of plucked nails, ears, fingers & toes

for years the ghost house is invisible in plain sight,
masked while the neighbors go on hanging laundry,

---

* *Al-hafla,* meaning "the party," is what torturers call the initial act of torture. The torturers blindfold
and collectively beat, rape, and abuse the newly imprisoned activists/artists/racial minorities for anywhere from six to twenty-four hours.

to dry, quickly, before the coffee boils over,
stirring warm sour dough & whistling hamza al din's tune,

about a bird whose addresses are dreams
etched into beating hearts—oblivious, that just next door,

that very tune is your last anchor, a realm
between death's cliff & the flesh-tattered

dentures of afterlife's shore,

by the end of the song
& before the coffee boils,

you are dead

& you are many men
& many father & sons & beloveds

& i do not know your names.

the ghost who lived

only when your torturer is certain beyond a
doubt that he severed your spirit from your
body, does he consider releasing you—ghost—
now emaciated & battered, to stagger into a
broken world

    to roam the streets as spectacle, to wear,
in your mangled skin the government's power
over its citizens, in your disfigurations, yes, the
power to manufacture & disperse death, but
alongside it is something more gruesome than
annihilation of life: the government's power to
extend the line between life & death into a
treacherous sea with no bridge over which to
cross, neither alive nor dead

   he blindfolds you, drives you to a crowded
location & throws you into the street with
nothing but the bloody clothes on your back,
tells you that agents will watch your every
move, that you must pray five times a day, that
you must start working as a spy,

           or they will return for you,
for you, this means only one thing, to fold
yourself into a boat over the nile's shoulder

ghost takes shots

after months, you limp your way home,
& on the way come up with a story to tell your wife

you cannot tell her about the rape,
the mock execution & failed kidney

you come up with another story for your mother
& notice onlookers plunged knee deep

in the fear of you, but you are barely here
& not wanting to be a ghost, the ugliness

that terrifies all others into sewing
their lips together before dreaming

your mother demands to know
why you are a walking corpse

you tell her that you have been away
on a work trip, you do not eat

& when you cannot find words,
the bitter milk of the ghost house curdles

in the soft spot between your cranium
& spine, settles as a silent foam,

your daughter walks now, & you reach
for another shot, until child & mother are gone

if you do not begin collaborating as a spy
they will come back to snatch you

so you wait for a booklet with a blue stamp,
pack your life into a single suitcase

swaying in the plane's underbelly,
after take-off, memory's chisel gently chips

away every dream you had, until revolution
is dust now, until your future is weak in the knees

eventually the plane lands
in a place where the trees wear needles

a country where everything spills over,
tears, whiskey, memory,

your wounds simmer down to a white
frothing puss & the snow falls

with the same silent grace,
as your wife reading the paper,

scratching the back of her knee
with the point of her big toe

& you reach for another shot

build a home out of skin

now i have no address
& every day
try to build a home out of skin
& bones
without bleeding out

i move into a crowded room
& mop the floor
so someone will have a reason
to keep me around

one day i am nauseous
with loss

& paint
with a stick of cinnamon
the memory of gone country
into the doors

& mark
with my knuckles
latitudes of displacement
along the dry wall

i paint joy,
it is brown & streaked

it is a birthmark
with bloodshot eyes

running through the house
like the nile overflowing
in the season of nearby rains

moya zargaa (n. blue water, drinking water)

at home i drink from al nil,
en route, i sip the mediterranean's water grave

in armeika, i do not know the origin of water
while weeping for home, i lick the ocean's callous

water womb with the roar of a thousand tongues
& a hammer old as the sky

ancestor's fistula crimsons the waves
into tight curls, or DNA, a carved lute, rippled skin

her spine is the pestle that grinds my mortal ear
to a fine beat, cartilage & plasma rain, she hums

from below the waves, i wonder, is it music
if it daggers stars into my neck?

or goose bumps, when the dead beneath
this skin sit-up in their sleep all at once

& make drum of my flesh? name it homage,

the beat calling with the force of palm
on taut fascia, my great-aunt, swallowed by the sea,
my unnamed, unborn nieces,

this is how to survive

hunted   &   haunted:

walk with one hand on the womb
& the other pressing memory like a rose

in a fist, back to water, the nile's creased neck,
gorgeous black canvas, the infant's thick lips

twisting into a field of fuchsia, irises of a lost country,
window of a mouth, born wet with sideways rain

bint zargaa (n. a blue girl; a dark-skinned child)

i tell allah, drop me a rope, part 1:

first day I arrive, I sayin allah to drop me a rope

next day I wake up

    with a boat

    where yesterday   there was a   hole

    months   before   I speakin
    a language   of rock

    it tryin   breakin   mine teeth

next year, i hearin a child in me
& i sayin allah to drop me two rope

i feel i am warm milk with honey
the day baby he breakin the water
my mother comin with plane
she sew jasmine flower into my finger
she sayin birth of a bikir
make small small the song of vein

    yes   maybe   i hittin   the doctor

        & from deep   & blood   i birth

    a flower   with eyes   & a cry

        in color   of fig   waiting in tree long long time

    purple/black   my heart   is our song   is my son

but my mother sayin to me, *look, look!*
lisaanu maqsoom, *the boy he havin split tongue!*

amatu

fur of snow on a long black braid, wool socks
& the plastic tongue of amatu's shibshib

clicking from the 83L stop to Halal Market

where she sells baskaweet for twenty bills
& a wind blows through her wild flower

print qamees, the kind she bought in Cairo
to sell under the plastic bag canopy at Suq Omdruman,

this is how she afforded the cost of divorce,
being a single mother in Khartoum,

until one day she tucked kisses
into her children's children's palms

& promised to return with green cards
so soon no one would have time to miss her

but the ticket did not take her
to the promised destination, instead,

armeika was a concussion to years
of wide-eyed nights in the basement

swaying to the quran's melody, weaving
her morning breath to a fine thread of grey hair,

she licks her thumb & caresses scripture as if
it is her daughter's fever-drenched scalp

i come home from school to find her baking
baskaweet yansoon, which i dip in milk,

tallying expenses on the back of receipts,
her eyes leap like a seesaw

trapped midair & unmoved by anything
lighter than the pain splitting her

from herself, sensing a witness, stories rise
like golden ghee at the dough's surface

i lean into the oven for warmth
& she begins to untangle herself
with as many words as the tea has cloves

before big government man paid your father
to tally prison suicides in american jails

he was a boy, not knowing english, or even
his own alphabet, he plundered landfills like a rabid dog

carrying me on his back, age of nine,
your father holding the small intestines of radios

& aorta of bicycles, to melt, to sell to blacksmiths
to buy, before returning home, the evening fava beans

did he have shoes? i ask amatu
& slice half-baked *beskaweet* dough

why carry me if we had shoes?
anyhow, haven't you ever wondered

about your father's hands?
in the landfill, the flames roasted his hands

my brother was aflame with the scent of barbeque,
 & my mouth watered, that is how hungry we were

amatu feeds the oven more dough,
her eyes are bloodshot, i do the math,

going at ten bills a pack, she'll never
bring her daughters to amreika

two hours to dawn she is low on faith & sugar,
amatu taps nine fingers, lost one recently
at a beef factory in Khartoum

the second time they deny her asylum,
she grows quiet for months, & one day,
not telling anyone, boards a plane home

the glass   & he rained

for my dear friend Sharif.   January 2006, Magdeburg, Germany

the police report states   your mother's throat resembles the desert
shortly before 7:30 A.M.   when she makes the eighth
international call & hollers

nazis chased Sharif on his way to school,
the youth climbed   *into a building, up the stairs*
all sixteen flights
& his wings   *pushed him through a closed window*
spread wide, he jumped   *the glass & he rained*

the wrinkled woman on the first floor
was plucked from a beige dream by   *my boy*
wailing   *fell sixteen flights*
& still breathing, heaving, he could've lived but

the old woman dialed the police to say   *they ran him over with a car*
█████ ████ ██ █████   as such
the police report states: *immediate death*
heart petrified upon first kiss of   mangoes & figs rot the sea within your
cranium against   mother's floods
uproots moons from the sky's glistening injury

scarlet snow & my boy's scalp
braided with tire marks,
the asphalt's chapped lips
unleashed his flesh from his skeleton   *I identified him by his shoes.*
his teeth & blood lukewarm

you are nine feet underground,
the police verdict: *suicide*   your mother, nine feet under water,
drains the bedrooms, a bucket each dawn

i tell allah, drop me a rope, part 2:

allah, I beggin you, please drop me a rope,
I done livin dis country, I done livin dis world

my boy he go to jail beecoz he havin split tongue
he havin accent in all language

[ajnabi   ESL   maqsoom
thug   maa'wuja   hood
taqeel   bridge   lajnaa

t   o   n   g   u   e]

allah, how come you makin his life a test
to livin two address, two world, with only one mouth?

he just a boy
my son, he sayin the bismilih al-rahman
al-rahim before he eatin

he sayin *thank you miss & eskusme officer*
he sayin *is kinda scary the way you pointing your gun at me*

then he sayin, *yes sir, my name is* [   ]

allah, please, I beggin, tell my son,
the sun at night still bleed in gold

today they make small small
the song of his vein, a reservoir

in the jail cell, a red mirror
for this country
                              25

allah, I beggin you, please drop me a rope,
I leavin dis country, I leavin dis world

the day we bring him home from jail

why would you do this to your mother?

tell me, what is the word for when the voice
you have not heard in years ushers the [s]weep

is the ocean's palm crunching
brother's cheek in her jaw?

we bring you home to mama's red eye explosion
her grief pours down his shirt, seeing this

i can't help but remember the day, a decade ago

the phone card cut out
    not enough funds, she said

                       * beep
                       * beep, click

or because it is the season of sandstorms
perhaps the connection is weak?   i suggested

but she collapsed on the stairwell
& the groceries   kissed   every step
from the top of the stairs
to the bottom

this is when she suspected her father,
my jidu, allahyarhamu, had passed,

but the phone call did not come
for another three days

her eldest brother's voice
was the only confirmation she needed
to split like the gungulez fruit

to dry up, as baobab meat must, to make
the tart white juice that raises the skin on the tongue

meanwhile you are out on probation

jidu's cornea have long since decomposed in the desert heat

& you are quivering like the nile's long long skirt

crossing the ocean,
this is not what anyone expected

to stare into the eye of the sink & think
this is it, this is what it's come to

the marriage, ten years fil qurba,
the girls & the newborn

one day a wife to a doctor,
suddenly a widow in a strange land
or curdled milk, turning in on myself,

a cold murmur, i pass down the drain
through the sputtering jaw

in our tradition a widowed woman
does not leave the house for forty days

believe me, if i were where i belong
there would be no fast grief

folded up on the dry tongue of a sofa
begging gravity for mercy

choking on armeika's fishhook fist
coiled in my vocal chords

if i were home my sisters would cook
while i sit in the sun & wring the neck of a chicken

for a moment its dwindling pulse matched to mine
for a moment death kneading life

seeing the sun through my palm, I would wonder
is my blood translucent because the ocean is drowning me from the inside out?

i would hand our daughter the limp bird & say
pluck it bare so that today death can also feed you

our child halfway to woman, halfway to orphan

if we were home
the whole town would be
a drum of sobs, the wail's plucked
sorrow, like smoke, would flow
to smolder in you, in me, a borderless pain
that dissolves the verge between us, here,

to restrain the winter's damp Sahara breath,
but i am not there, in my ears the sirens echo

by the third day there are no mourners at the door
in this armeika where time is weighted & rationed

like sugar during the occupation, scanty
for the price of its harvest

no time to live, no time to die, in this country
where a casket is half a year's salary

this far from home, who will bring the girls to school?
who will buy the groceries? or pay the rent?

i don't have days, not forty days
to sieve through my marrow, nostril deep,

& return the scorpions to the dessert
so I lock the door behind me

& take the kids for happy meals,
we have only the anchor of each other's grief

my feet abloom with blisters, wild thorns
& our infant boy needs to feed   at my sweetness

                              dehydrated
                              white dust
                              he chokes
& i am a broken cassette,
my song's black tape strewn about the house

there is no melody here any longer
just a tangled stutter

how can i reel my intestines in
past the fishhook in my throat

my family said go make a life in the land of opportunity

but did not say   we will be too far to taste your agony
did not say   it is possible to die so far from your roots

only strangers will come to your funeral

smoke

when I hear the women gossip
that they have seen me leave the house

that I could not go forty days without chasing a new man,
my rage captures each vein

i know, my love, that you know, it is not true

i learn to pluck the eye of the heart's savage pain:
touch a match to my inner forest

feel the bark curl from the years,
watch decades rewind until

my skin is a coat of black moths
gone to chase the moon

until one morning
the infant is a fetus

& you, my love, stand in the tub
rinsing smoke from your hair

mango skull

you see, this is not what anyone expected

to be a flat tire bearing the brunt of the street
hammered to the teeth

i remember yesterday   when i was a man

a rose festering   through the kidney of
atbara jail   a single thorn in the trachea
hymn of my hunger

before yellow years passed me in this cab
before the college diploma turned to debris
& my siblings watched the dust gather
& sucked their teeth as if to ask

with what voice does dignity cry

at the grave of her splintered father?

*

i remember yesterday   1970-something

dignity   a fava bean dinner in a jail cell
locked up
for counter-dreaming
with the sun in our teeth

i remember something   1980-dignity

just yesterday   blood in the early hours
of morning, the fists of eight Muslim brothers
                              sprayed out my fractured skull
a parade of red upon the street

I remember yesterday   1990-nothing

                    omar al-bashir

submerged the left   left me no choice

flooded I fled west

all that for this

to drive a cab through streets i would not bleed for,
for bills that don't add up to match the rent,
amreika   a nation lynching my honor
with loopholes made for   another body

*

27 years later i tell you   [my daughter]

    before i fled Sudan i left my dreams at the bend of a
street, in the shade of a mango tree
        thinking, i'll be back before sunset

33

as soon as the hunt is over

my hair is grey now,
afro cropped short; bashir has a new palace
                              the street has a new name
                                    & the tree is gone
i swallow my teeth
on my knees, I dig
                              all is gone except the single
                                    white skull of a mango

          i gift you its seed

this pit

plant this remnant of a lost generation;
a dream that will outlive the gallows
                                    & every war

          plant it deep in your flesh
                                    without bleeding out

then, one day, my child,
          the sun shall shine
                    through the yellow scalp
                         of a mango
                              onto your tongue

homecoming after twenty years, 2010

this is the last season Sudan is one,
which is not to say it is the last time we northerners

will fail southerners [& westerners,
& anyone outside the capital, to keep the list brief]

this is the year i rupture, after twenty years,
my son sees me crying, & asks, *baba bitebki malak?*

& i point at the sidewalk & tell him,
this is where my cranium split

[& i feel it splitting again] *this is the prison
where i made chess figurines of mud*

this is where i was flogged for leading a protest

this is the year i will lose the thing
i gave my life protecting

the unity that is a long gone anecdote,
the justice hundreds died defending

this city is thick with the smoke of fish skin
sizzling in oil & an acquired taste, something sweet

& desperate that leaves my throat itching,
like cinnamon but not nearly as old,

the memory of what was, just thirty years ago, a nostalgia
my children are too young to savor

i explain to them, *it is not that i am unhappy*
for southern independence, but that our enemy is one

that our enemy has won by dividing us,
that despite everything, we have failed our kin

i wipe my overflow & watch an elderly donkey pull
across the sidewalk, a cart with a single wheel

this is the year i wish to join the sand that climbs into
the sky's lap to sleep, this land of impossible reminiscence

i fled grieving for my comrades & return grieving
so ugly a scar, this border silhouette of future displacement,

how i love both Sudans, north & south,
each having wrapped herself on the eve of independence

in an elegant cotton toab, now stiff with heat
in the year the breeze will bend the fabric's knees

in a truck climbing the left ventricle of omdurman's heart, three girls; two cut, one uncut

I.

on the toilet seat   *any given day*

labia stretched like
bubblegum in child fingers

bent over, I peer into myself   mahal albohl
translucent maroon eclipse

position mirror between the knees
excavate beneath   the hood
                                                                    loaded cunt
                                                                    no trigger
                                                                    no safety

                                          either
something was taken   or   something was left
                                          clitoris
                        cut   //   uncut
                no proof of what I can neither
forget   nor   remember

& no way to tell
having never seen

                                          a body beside my own splayed open

II.

in the kitchen   *winter 2008*

amatu cries from too much laughter

nine & a half fingers knead black seeds
into dough as she tells me (& I am a child):

> *at the hospital they had me believing I was*
> *the deceased at an open casket funeral*
>
> *a long line of doctors waiting a turn*
> *to lean in & snap a picture*
>
> *they spread my legs*
> *just to stare into me & cry*
>
> *& cry. ttte. can you imagine, they must've*
> *never seen a ugly thing their whole life*
>
> *if I could speak english I would've told them*
>
> *you must think my vagina is your mother's dead corpse hmm?*
> *ttte! who gave you permission to grieve a living thing unn?*

we laugh & laugh & laugh

in the kitchen
cuvier is the oilspill in my lungs

saartjie bartman is the ember before we know her name,
the nurses are ash under our fingernails

amatu pleats into herself
laughter & tears

how effortlessly & without noticing
they made a free day at the zoo of her

       black & breathing body

III.

at the barbeque   *spring 2010*

cousin fresh off the plane
breastfeeds her daughter
stirring sugar into black tea
& asks the other mothers

                where fil qurba does one find a doctor
                willing to perform the operation?

the girl crawls, grasping grass

& my blood is an underwater horse
hunting a burnt out star
with a net of its own sinews

IV.

in the operating room   *NTBR**

fists in impossible knots,
the doctor's oversize tweezers, the razor's
crimson rain on cloudless scrubs
splinters of a wail upstream three windpipes

what no one remembers:
which one of us; you, or she, or I,
laid splayed open on the operating table

when Amu ran through the door yelling, shaking

       touch her & I will kill you!

the two others having already been cut,
red wool crossing & uncrossing at our feet

---

* NTBR: not to be remembered

V.

in the back of Amu's truck   *minutes later*

climbing the left ventricle
of Omdurman's heart,
three girls; two cut, one uncut

& not a single tear, sudden the drought
of departure from childhood

three magnificent starched dresses
stiff with young sweat

& three girls trembling
at the interior waterfall's gaping mouth

the blood reaching its endless arm
through our cunts & down the street

VI.

hers is a body beside my own

                    opening

my waist
may as well be the banana tree
she climbed

barefooted child
thighs pressed to the bark
laughing her way to the fruit

holding a loaded cunt
as if it were the sugar cane's backbone
making a saccharine balm

for the wound
I can neither remember
nor forget

mine is a body
I do not own
opening

PAUL'S WHOLE VERSE

[1]Finally brethren,
The lover born on a Thursday,
whose flaws you can map out blindfolded
the easier-to-be-kinder-to stranger
the one who doesn't look, smell or sound like you
the known face who never acknowledges your eagle wings
the body in which you reside;
both on days you love it
and especially days you don't.

[2]whatever things are true,
Shifting weather blueprints
glee that travels through your body
like uncontrollable pee
pain that measures on a scale of 9.7
when the doctor asks, "how bad?"
love as a quiet fear that sharpens your mother wit

[3]whatever things are noble,
Ghana jollof
Your face before and after makeup
Voices that taste like ice cream on a humid day

[4]whatever things are just,
orgasms that make your legs twitch
bellies as full as breasts
brick roofs and linoleum floors
someone whose godliness glows from loving you

⁵whatever things are pure,
the way your soul yanks out of your body
when you're tickled
the unpretty laugh that
spills out of your mouth
the smelly fart you cannot believe
is being pushed out of your body
the unrighteous anger that clenches your jaw

⁶whatever things are lovely,
well grilled tilapia from your neighbour
as compensation for the loud music
warm fulfilling hugs that make you want to spill your truth
wanted silences
temporary pain when god gifts rejection letters
in preparation for a book deal

⁷whatever things are of good report,
60% discount on new leather brouges
paying what you owe without going broke
love as Papier-mâché

⁸if there is any virtue and if there is anything praiseworthy—
if it makes your insides tingle
if it makes the insides of others tingle
if it lulls the angst

⁹meditate on these things
let your life be the sermon
let your body be a vessel
sing out of tune about it

bruise, hemorrhage, revive

rewind the track.

BEFORE THE GAG

my mother calls me her dearest,
kisses my hand and squeezes it gently.
she swears I'm surviving solely on her prayers
because she's not convinced there's a quarter of enough food in my body.
not with all the hollow in my collarbones.

I have hit a roadblock in trying to use language to navigate my feelings.
the same words that pave way, stand in my way.
how do I distract myself from myself in order to free myself?
how do I use language against itself?
what comes after I have puked out the last sentence of distress?

mother said to eat a little more,
for *Will* shall take to *Strength's* heels.
so I buy time with unbalanced paragraphs and reluctant doodles,
wait for the pressure that sparks the gag reflex,
so I can retch it all out.

SPIT

January has been teaching me
that hurt can come from even the snuggliest spaces.
I'm reminded you are still
a sharp, blooming, flustered, selfish, reckless, gooey boy
I love—who has no desire to learn
                    to love me back in a language I understand.

I miss the boy you used to be;
shapelessness and angst leaves my body
                    and comes back homeless.
Wednesday evening we talk about news trending in Accra.
How it's the only thing that resembles home
but is still incapable of swallowing me whole,
                    and why I think you're full of shit sometimes.
We talk about your day and my day and everything,
but how you and the city are breaking my heart.

After minutes of silence, you ask what I'm thinking,
and I smile and say nothing
of the time we kissed,
                    how you thawed in my mouth.
It's like wanting to wrestle a child.

Our love is an incomplete elegy.
You dish out I-love-you's like there's a famine in your throat
and you have to ration them.
What's the English word for someone who still has hope
in lovers who cause too much anxiety?
                    Tell me so I can spit it out.

SUICIDE SARAH

There's something about you
that makes looking away impossible.
You're not what the world would label as pretty.
You're not soft and sweet and tender,
and all the butter words used to describe beautiful.
Your face is finely chiseled,
And your body stands out
like a nipple on a cold rainy night.

You're in love with a boy whose mother
left him on the stairs of her mother's house
to go follow a man who never loved her.
You're in love with a boy whose grandmother
saved his good clothes only for a father
who barely visited.
And so he's always waiting
for a big day, a big moment, a big reason,
before he gives you all of his love,
when he should be kissing
the spaces in between your toes.

You smoke on rooftops to take away the heartache.
You allow others to cut you
and get high off watching yourself bleed.
Men have been looking for God inside of you,
and you have been looking for God
in the faces of strangers who offer you their coat.
Everybody wants you at their parties because they know
you're as good at them as you are at blowjobs.

Everybody wants to drink with you.
Everybody wants to dance with you.
Everybody wants to fuck around with you.
But nobody wants to walk blindly
through the dark to help you find yourself.
Well, damn everybody.
Damn the calvary and damn the cross.
Damn the saints and damn the whores.
Damn the beggar down the street
who called you ugly because you wouldn't spare a coin.
Damn everybody!
Do they not know
that the sun borrows light from your fingertips?
Do they not know
that you give colour to the rose?
Do they not know
that your breath is studied by the highest of connois-
seurs
to make the best of perfumes?
There's something about you
that makes looking away impossible.

TAKE, EAT

I have left parts of myself on your son's body.
I whispered my name around his beautiful hollow
navel,
spent quality time inside his mouth,
kneaded my tongue against his.
I have tasted him,
tasted desire in the way his muscles lie
prostrate when my lips touch his
Sexual attraction only lasts 6 weeks.
It's been two years since we kissed:

Does the sign of the cross
Hands clasped.
Whispers amen.
It's time to eat.

SPURTING

3 a.m. is for sleeping soundly in the nook of my collarbone.
Instead, I'm talking with my eyes closed, waiting for you to give me reason

to still want to rest my leg between your butt cheeks twenty years from today.
How are you holding yourself from eating me up?

How do you not want me to oblivion?
How is my love for you leaving you both breathless and sane?

I kissed you a little too hard and a bit of your ego got stuck in my mouth.
So when I come up for air my tongue sounds like your language.

But my father taught me the best way for pride to thrive is when it blends in.
This speaking in tongues is familiar territory.

There's fertilizer in my spit,
and my grandmother's green thumb in my bones.

You must want to be with me on an 80% success rate.
I am not a gamble.

Be so sure of how transforming my love will be to your growth
                        because all this body knows how to do is to flare.

AND I'VE MASTERED THE ART OF RECEIVING HAND-OUTS BECAUSE I COME FROM THIS PLACE

I am hungry for a love my country cannot afford.
I want a love
that will buffer my mistakes even before I commit them;
a love that has mapped out the possibilities of my existence
and made room for each one of them;
a love that doesn't need me to clamour to identify as black too
just so I can swim in the opportunity pool;
a love that doesn't even need me to have an archive of pain
to be worthy of inclusion.
I want a love
that doesn't need me to work like there's two of me
in this body just to be visible;
a love that doesn't require me to be
both pregnant and doula
trying to pull a nirvana out of my ass just for being different.
I want a love
that doesn't require me to be ridiculously multifaceted
in order to have a fraction of an equation at being equipped for survival;
a love that doesn't wait for another suitor to sing the praises of my genius
before recognizing my worth,
or worse, only after I'm dead.
I am hungry for a love my country cannot afford,
the way white lusts for a backdrop to outshine.

BULKY BUILDING

My lovers have stemmed from branches
broken off strong platonic relationships,
and when the romance bleeds out,
or gets rusty,
or croons like a faulty car engine that no mechanic can repair,
the friendship wobbles like weak knees.
and we use short answers and distractions and distance
to patch the feelings of despair.
I have stretched myself wide in anticipation of love

FORGIVENESS

There's something about the way people leave
that makes you want to bottle who you are
and keep it safe from the world.
You have a brave face that only lets you rent it
for public appearances and old relationships.
You plough the road of failing friendships
where awkwardness is an easy language.
And forgive everybody but yourself.
Forgive yourself for convincing yourself
you will never know a greater love;
for creating this architecture of doom
and living underneath its leaking truth,
forgive yourself,
for you are a breath of fresh air,
forgive yourself,
for there is overflowing love
lining up to engulf you.

NOT SO MUCH

In answering a question on recharging one's self,
a ~~male~~ poet once said:

"Being tired in your body is great,
being tired in your mind, not so much"

With all due respect sir,
you must not know shit about a body that's tired.

Because have you seen a body unravel?
skin burning with the softest touch,

scabbed wounds and fractured bones,
Pain hanging out your eyes like loose door handles,

legs failing like a broken home,
hope an unfamiliar looking dude,

healing slower than the time
it takes my country to pay its pensioners.

You must not know shit about a body that's tired,
and maybe that's a good thing to not know.

LET IT BE

I have been fretting over things that God shakes his head at
toying with faith as if it were a disappearing act.
One minute I'm full of it,
the next, I don't exactly know the shape of it.
I fret over now and tomorrow,
giving myself and God a headache.
Spoon feed myself faith,
and come up hungry again.
I have taken up all the space on my mother's prayer sheet
and the happiness of those I love takes up all of mine.
At the end of day, we're both in God's ears
saying let it be.

BLOOM

I could write about how bodies are the most malleable things.
I could fill a page with how pain leaves words hanging in your throat.
I could write a poem about the way people soften up
when their lovers kiss the small of their back.
I tried to write something musical about my city and I did not know
where to start.
When I walk through south of Labadi, the streets are bursting with an
abundance of heritage;
I can tell from the way the dark-skinned woman with the y-shaped scar
on her left leg
scrubs her baby, that she is a woman who believes in redemption.

Two boys are moving like they've got too much rhythm in their bodies
and not enough time to dance it out.
A little girl sucks on a lollipop, spits in her hand and offers it
to her small sister who gleefully licks it up.
They have a look on their face that tells that they know
what they're doing is ridiculous and sweet and terrible;
they know wrong isn't right, but they do it anyway.
On the pavement, a porridge seller is giving out smiles
like they are Amens to needy requests.

A man is telling a stranger that he doesn't even like porridge,
but the way she throws her head back when she drinks it down,
does things to him.
And her laughter tumbles down like the hollow echo of a djembe.
What he doesn't know is that this is her first laugh in days.
Old Ms. Atta has a tight lipped smile as if
her mouth is holding on to sins yet to be forgotten,

and when she sings akwaaba ɔdɔ, she means it.
These people teach me,
that if you are from Accra and you are placed anywhere in
the world,
there's no way you won't know how to bloom.

SEPIA

My parents love in sepia
a thing brewed from the slow decay of a new sprout,
seasoned and mature enough to have a feeling named after it;
teaching me that decay is not always synonymous to rot—
only a point on the growth curve.
Because this brown has seen tender and folded,
this brown has been foolish and free,
this brown has feigned sufficiency to make way for enough;
this brown with its share of pain and scars,
knows how to love the glow out of any sun.

SHAMEPLANT

They say poets are the only people who chase after pain.
They sit at the edge of the city with their arms stretched out,
like beggars asking for alms,
because their art becomes such a perfection
in their pain that they should live in it.
But I swear to god I would rather house you in my skin
if it meant putting my art at risk.
Loving so hard that brain cannot comprehend body.
Isn't it both beautiful and strange
how we're so convinced we will never love again
when our hearts have been broken?
Yet, each time, we break our promises to ourselves.
And that's where you found me.
A Shameplant wide open,
so damn sure that I never wanted to love again.
When you met me, I had become a war town,
tongue like a woman's wrath,
teeth holding lips firmly grounded like a fenced wall,
prison keys of a dead inmate behind both ears,
lips tasting like food with too much salt,
body sagging under the weight of reality
threatening to mimic my nightmares.
And you kissed the tremble out of my lower lip.
The moon learnt how to arc its back
from studying the perfect shape of your eyes.
You summoned poems from my fingers
when everyone else was asleep.
And I don't even mean to sound cliché
but the only way things can graduate to the school of cliché

is if they are true.
And you were the truth.
And God, how I loved you.
But you left.

And grief struck me dumb for my inability to make you stay.
And I stood like an opening prayer
before the pulpit on bended knees.
Hoping that God would hear how much I wanted you back
and whisper it into your ear.
What was pride?
I would shove it under my feet and declare my love for you.
What would I not do for you?
I would sing your name like a hymn,
I would change the order of the months if it made you happy,
I would clean your molars out with my tongue,
and spit their message on your tongue,
for your lips to preach the gospel of your greatness to the world.
I would lift my hands up to keep the sun from setting for you.
I would be the Amen at the end of your sermon.
Let it be.
Let me be.
Let us be.
But you left.

And I reek so much of pain that two houses away
the neighbours swear they can smell the stench.
I remember when I told you I loved you,
you kissed the words off my tongue
and acted like it was a treasure.
Yet today you treat it like the corny translation

of an odd scripture by a hungry preacher.
It is terrifying how many good qualities
you can project unto the people you love.
You tell me you love me still, even before I ask you.
You love me, but not enough to stay.
You moved out of town and wouldn't let me on the bus.
I need someone who knows how to stay.

A GOOD DAY FOR REDEMPTION

Dear Nalorm,

Now that we both agree that our twenties are home to ruin, our bodies have become liberation grounds for redemption. The late night calls, the salt-laced shots, the outrageous twenty cedi taxi fare for a ten minute journey after 1am, the tipsy laughter, the pitiful ritual of guilt-tripping old lovers by disappearing, whole man-parts drilled into our black holes in search of missing orgasms. We've both been pretending we've seen the light at the end of the goddamn awful tunnel. But we were so eager to claim this adulthood title we forgot we hadn't grown up. Truth be told, if I could have the cockiness with which naivety knew your body's address and rented space there in your adolescence, I would snatch it. The freedom that comes with not knowing enough about the cruelty of the world to remember to be ashamed of your body. The short length of time it takes to get ready to step out because you're not pinching or poking or burrowing like your skin is target practice for greenhorns. An old lover once told me he was sitting on an undiscovered gold mine because he was dating a flat chested girl who he hoped would become voluptuous in future. And my face lit up because I believed myself an undiscovered gold mine. You can blame everything on youth if you're drunk enough, his illegal touch, food spiced with low self-esteem, a body that doesn't know how to forgive itself. Nalorm, my high school dormitory was built on an old cemetery. The way I see it, either we're feeding off the dead, or dead things were laid here to rest so we could live each day new. The Old Testament God promised joy in the morning, but there's no way of telling time in dark tunnels. So any day is a good day for redemption.

ACKNOWLEDGEMENT

With grateful acknowledgment to *Litro* magazine, which provided a platform for me to publish the poem "Spit," which is included in this collection.